Exploring Earth's Resources

Using Rocks

Sharon Katz Cooper

www.raintreepublishers.co.uk

Visit our website to find out more information about **Raintree** books.

To order:

 Phone 44 (0) 1865 888112

 Send a fax to 44 (0) 1865 314091

 Visit the Raintree Bookshop at **www.raintreepublishers.co.uk** to browse our catalogue and order online.

First published in Great Britain by Raintree, Halley Court, Jordan Hill, Oxford OX2 8EJ,
part of Harcourt Education.
Raintree is a registered trademark of Harcourt Education Ltd.

© Harcourt Education Ltd 2007
The moral right of the proprietor has been asserted.

Editorial: Isabel Thomas, Sarah Chappelow and Vicki Yates
Design: Michelle Lisseter
Illustrations: Q2A Solutions
Picture Research: Erica Newbery
Production: Duncan Gilbert
Originated by Modern Age
Printed and bound in China by South China Printing Company

10 digit ISBN 1 406 20617 2
13 digit ISBN 978-1-4062-0617-3
11 10 09 08 07
10 9 8 7 6 5 4 3 2 1

British Library Cataloguing in Publication Data
Cooper, Sharon Katz
  Using rocks. – (Exploring Earth's resources)
  1. Stone – Juvenile literature
  I. Title
  333.8'55

  ISBN – 13: 9781406206173
  ISBN – 10: 1406206172

A full catalogue record for this book is available from the British Library.

Acknowledgements
The publishers would like to thank the following for permission to reproduce photographs: Alamy pp. **6** (blickwinkel), **10** (Interfoto Pressebildagentur), **18** (Dennis Macdonald), **19** (ImageState), **21** (image 100); Corbis pp. **4** (Robert Harding World Imagery), **16**, **17** (Ecoscene); Geoscience Features Picture Library pp. **14** top and bottom, **15**; Getty Images pp. **9** (Photodisc Red), **12**, (photodisc), **13** (Jack Dykinga); Photolibrary **20** (Brandx Pictures); Science Photo Library pp. **5** (Mauro Fermariello), **11** (Doug Martin); Still Pictures pp. **7**

Cover photograph reproduced with permission of Getty Images (Medio Images).

Contents

Some words are shown in bold, **like this**.
You can find them in the glossary on page 23.

What are rocks?

The Earth is made of rocks.

Rocks are underneath soil and grass. They are underneath water.

Rocks are a **natural resource.**

Natural resources come from
the Earth.

What are rocks made of?

Rocks are made of different **minerals**.

Minerals are natural materials that are not alive.

iron

The minerals in a rock change how it looks and feels.

Iron is a mineral. Rocks with iron in them are hard.

magma

Liquid rock deep inside the Earth is called **magma**.

Magma cools and hardens slowly inside the Earth.

granite

It forms rocks such as granite.

How are rocks formed?

magma

Sometimes **magma** pours out
of volcanoes. It becomes hard
very quickly.

obsidian

It forms rocks such as obsidian.
Obsidian is very smooth, like glass.

Wind and water break big rocks into smaller pieces.

Stones and pebbles are small pieces of rock.

Soil and sand are tiny pieces of rock.

Layers of soil and sand pile up and become hard. They can form a new kind of rock.

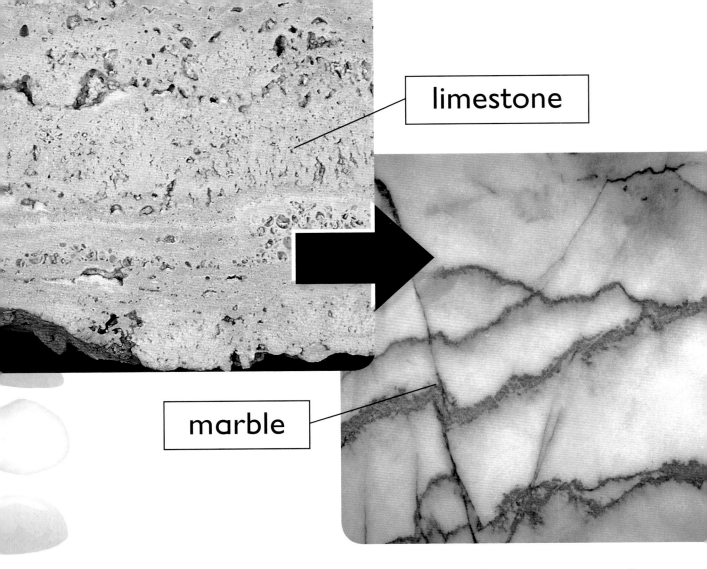

limestone

marble

Heat and **pressure** can change rock.

Very hot temperatures change limestone into marble.

14

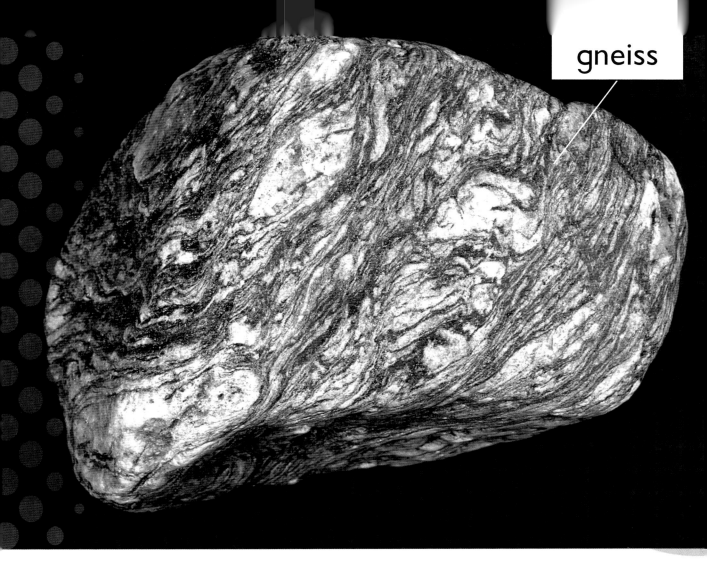

gneiss

Rocks like gneiss have very flat layers.

Pressure formed these layers in the rocks over time.

Where do we find rocks?

Some rocks are easy to find.

They can be cut from the side of mountains or cliffs.

Some rocks are only found deep in
the Earth.

We have to dig down to get them out.

How do we use rocks?

We use small pieces of rock to make roads.

A road has many layers of rock underneath.

We use big pieces of rock to build things. Marble is a strong rock.

Buildings made of marble last a long time.

We use very soft rocks to make plaster.

Plaster makes walls smooth.

Some rocks are very hard and beautiful. They are rare.

We use them to make jewellery.

Rock collection

Scientists who study rocks are called geologists.

You can be a geologist in your own classroom or garden. Look for different types of rocks. Use the key to find out what they are.

What does it feel like?

Smooth

Rough

What does it look like?

What does it look like?

No grains or layers, like glass

Flat grains or layers

Layers of different colours

Flat grains or layers

It is an **igneous rock!**

It is a **metamorphic rock!**

It is a **sedimentary rock!**

It is a metamorphic rock!

Glossary

 **igneous rock** type of rock made when a volcano explodes

 **magma** liquid rock under the Earth's surface

 **metamorphic rock** type of rock made when other rock gets very hot under the ground

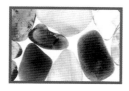 **mineral** a non-living material from the Earth

 **natural resource** a material from the Earth that we can use

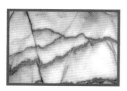 **pressure** pushing or squeezing on something

 **sedimentary rock** type of rock made when mud, sand, or sea creatures fall to the bottom of the sea

Index

Titles in the *Exploring Earth's Resources* series include:

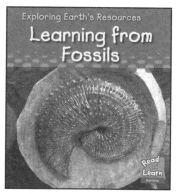

Hardback 1-406-20623-7

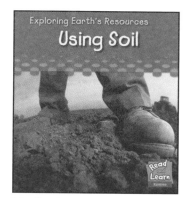

Hardback 1-406-20618-0

Hardback 1-406-20617-2

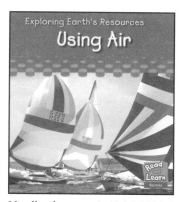

Hardback 1-406-20621-0

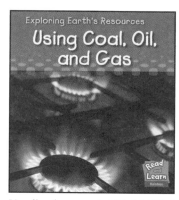

Hardback 1-406-20622-9

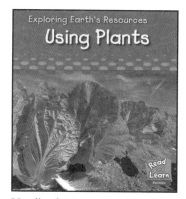

Hardback 1-406-20619-9

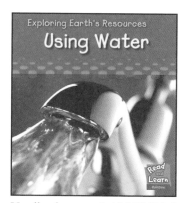

Hardback 1-406-20620-2

Find out about the other titles in this series on our website www.raintreepublishers.co.uk